Manual for Extinction

Manual for Extinction

caroline manring

The National Poetry Review Press
Aptos, California

The National Poetry Review Press
(an imprint of DHP)
Post Office Box 2080, Aptos, California 95001-2080

Printed in the United States of America
Published in 2014 by The National Poetry Review Press

ISBN 978-1-935716-33-4

Cover artwork:
Tyson Grumm
Odo the Last Dodo
All rights reserved. (c) 2012
www.facebook.com/TysonGrumm

TABLE OF CONTENTS

Acknowledgments

How to Go Extinct

A bird's mouth is its gape.
As when
young beg.

No one let us go awry;
we just got some heavy focus on
& failed to write
home.

We found a pasture
& delivered ourselves
into it
unprepared. We found

things happen
before our hands
untwist

the wire.

How to Number the Abundant Things
While They Are Still Abundant

At the field-   days of desire there was
a booth for shooting skylarks.

Sometimes rhetoric   is just
a lone   stud horse.

Three forests,   one untouched
one logged   one
razed

sustained   the same
birds but not the same
beetles

we must make endings meet
this is a place   called Earth

I hurried   to the fence
& said
I too wanted

a horse

Monster

Suicide mice
did bombings
on me as I lay. And all that death

to split seams.
Penultimate, there was quietude, certainty.

Then bits, noise, a gulping chamber.
I trace my pulped edges, brushing

aside the bodies of allies to see
their success. Fingers guess,

dig to measure
the cavity's perimeter: ribs pulled off their charges:

ventricles and drumlins, an esker.

How to Assess Damage

I never dealt
in hundred dollar bills before.

Are you the rake or the coals?
Pleased to break you.

And the fox was tricked and fell
into the creamy water but I
don't deal in middles so I can't
say how.

Holding
this pose is brutal and the
cello begins to sound
like a shuttle with a known
hairline fracture
entering
anyway

No one listened
to the engineers
their perfect
equations
that put the debris
right through
your eye

How to Care for Lab Animals

Fortune has it   the very mammal you
-'ve selected makes just such in-
cisions. You can
-'t get this kind
of stock any
-where else in
(t)his kingdom. We're (going
the way of) the seed
-bank.

Rights to re-
product
-ive process
-es waver like half-
mashed moths. We are so
full of (g)race   the fall   the
end   looks

like just an
-other soft descent on
-to a con-
vex
-ity. The con
-sequent off-
spring grow
on clear-
cut coffee plant
-ations, syn
-onyms for the crop's self-

evident you-
th,

pro
-duct of: fun-
ction/ prudence/ re-
verence, so help
them god. I
-'m is-
suing a par

-don for this & any
moment that

lets
you live
in image.

The Cartographer's Children Go Without Shoes

A fossil is deciding
whether to save us.
(Archaeopteryx, say less.)

There are days of sore veins.

I displayed, I displaced, many feathers.

The rest is murmuring hooves,
the murmur-broker's bread.

Save the method.
My clear hope of stopping

has woken & toed the line
of fallen peaches.

How to Keep Your Eyes on Your Own Mat

It would have been better
if he'd hung from a wire in this grief of a city—

just planar iterations, space
& its companion calf.

There's an armory
or town hall if you're fragile

& stupid enough to home,
pigeon-style—
beautiful, aristocratic, & as likely to die
as fruit. That's where limbs sign

off, forage elsewhere for a new ancestor,
& the thorax, forsaken, asks simply

"am I invited?"

One must
sometimes come
to the runt
which once
released
races out

to slake
this cold that is
the hunger of reindeer.

How to Factory Farm

Created & stung, the body's task
was to be middling,
where it could remain safe.
So the body set its heart
on becoming a government

with enough bad back-story
to make a good novel.
Ruby Foreman's job was to
pick up chicken heads.

She forgot how many she'd held
at the end of each day because
numbers numbed her.
No matter how many times you count
you still have to cram

your tenderness down their throats
so they can die well,
as with a prayer or a flash of heavy silver
from the generous, heaving water.

How to Believe You Are a Founding Father

No one has to wait in line for long.

You may be shocked by the way
real organs feel in your hands.

You will find your life
is neither yours nor empty.
Putting us all in one place

accents the lack of planning.

When you're not measuring or masoning
you begin to apprehend meaning:

blow-up lawn ornaments,
deer that fall when they cross,
alpacas gathering

by the fence.

How to Live on the Plains

I want to haul myself onto earthly flotsam
not anything too intimate

just me & some geese
scattering by
on course.
When we are arranged by crop

you can see we are a toothy,
forever naked, rag-tag lot.

There are hands
deft enough to find diagnostic
sweetnesses.

Untrained, we & our examiners
go wanly wading,

never a crossing
to speak of. But here in my heart

there is no accidental pony.

How to Get Out of Inverted Staff Pose

. And you can't be anything other than whole

, Then the busting of the ribs

; Then that was imaginary

. Ask a partner to tip you over

, If a beast can cross a meadow

, If you cannot be ruined

, If your body is a blade,

If you cannot be ruined,

If a beast can cross a meadow,

Ask a partner to tip you over.

Then that was imaginary;

Then the busting of the ribs,

And you can't be anything other than whole.

Hydraulic Fracture

Name the blaze.
Bear it in a box.

My father's tourniquet
makes an oarlock.

Racked with possession

we row on land.

How to Get to Wounded Knee

We dangle a pledge
before the gathering sky

The drunk stands still as a post
& the sky begins to whine
like a huge hurt dog

Oaths flap unreceived
their guarantors even
having gone

Here
is a Heath Hen egg

Go
ahead, try

try to photograph it

The Wiffleball Hall of Fame

There they are without
                their bodies,
                          beautiful as anything.

Behind them, mute teams of heavy
                horses beam
                      like climbing beans.

A loose flock, children
                      as seen through green glass
                            compose an entire season,

have ponies & grudges. Salamanders deftly
                tagged with thread
                        to good church clothes.

Tough field competitors
                high-step over hedges
                      at a suicidal distance.

How to Be Extinct

All the banging became coherent
like subtitles
siphoning ocean
into a bowl.

What can we subtract
to expose substrate like
a billion-dollar tomb?

Sometimes, you.
Then I see the footprints in the dregs
are avian, or a moth's.

Often we remove with partial success
the competing heartbeat.
Have you ever spread someone's ashes
with your hands?

I take mules into the
stable of my heart & wonder
why there are so precious few escapes.

Figure A: shroud

(if) she knew who could stand in the ring
after a hard whack to the face
they (would) become it

each month less lucid
blinks at the city

               idiom   of addendum

law   as sorrow   & vittles
                            many thanks

for your sweet body,

           nothing's cleaved   in two   though

pots of herbs

         smashed

               by passersby
          stand
          terra-cotta-less
      roots still
         in form
              (like a woman's
hands at spinning

or plaiting or at

        the making of kings)

in rosemary
& orange dust
six days til the trash
man's notice:
        text

quick as the one-year life
of the wild kinglet   which in

        captivity
lives   nine

How to Play the Most Beautiful Quartet
in the World

To step on a fox tooth or a fish bone
on the railroad tracks & not know
what it is
opens one vein
in an evening that wasn't
there before. One more
place for blood to go. My sister is not the queen
but she is one such place. In every
student there's a teacher causing problems.
Like a statue you sat on & didn't have the heart
to let anyone know. You stay seated, present
at the bridal shower, like the shuttle launch
the Mars fanatic somehow forgot to calendar
but it happens, and brightly, too. Rescued or not,
with binoculars
one can learn a bird's field-marks all right.
Though one may never be great
at reading the sky.

How to Align Planets

Ruth's stand-partner
turns pages. After
the partner's death
rooms open. Never mind
planets.

A person parses
the non-negotiable act
clearly in units
no one's ever used.

Outside the mourning room, which looks
so much like
the living room, syzygy takes place
as the wariangle takes a frozen grape.

Within, we hear a steady flock of bodies—
right down to the loyal Maltese,
if we are to continue making
a living of this.

1. The Call

Grace befit
Me meat

Wi'out,
Wi'in
A wheel:

I ring
To call,
To puncture steel.

Arise,
Elite, oh
Bloodied feet—

2. The Fall

Th' stoke: abide.
Torrent unspoke.
Waylaid among
Thy ribald stars

Sin fact *sin* farce
As hem or doll
Wi' plant in hand
Did fluttered fall.

Ye aye in bloom.
To grist thy mill
I hanged, an' hung,
I wa' the kill'd—

In winded best
In windin' chest
In tumblet- hair
In sadlong stare.

3. Calling the Kye[1]

Aye, ho! Traum up, up on
Sing slash, an' oh, an' on.
He brings it Told
An' his tall hold
We find our flung
Our dark be sung
Tae on, tae up,
Tae act a sun
A land, a lord,
Me flayed, among.

4. Wee One Watches from Time Tae Come

A canticle, pray,
The dungeons stray
Out o' doors,
Yea, they come
A-rut among
And side-slip taut.

The wonders fought!
For plank's a mistin'
An' brine's contrivin'
An' battlin' spits on
Mumsie, Pa.
They canna know
The kye[1] is aye
Wandrin' long
The hoary brae.
See, they canna luve
In fields sae blue
The blue betakes
Their gee & haw.
Leave'm their awe,
Their brawn, ye bairn.

5. Tryst

Sop
An'
Tryst
For
Grip,
Not
Bliss.
Me
Rain
Ha'
Hung
O'er
Girders.
The

_____
[1] cows

Saw
Whose
Teeth
Did
Knaw,
The
Brig
Did
Hold
An'
Braw.
So
Placet
So
Strung—ah—
Be
Heat
Be
Gone!—

6. Nightwatch to the Swallowing Sea

Mem'ry welding
Fortune smelt me.
Creaks th' bed mold,
Single lesson:
Hold me, knee me.
Iron bleed thee,
Iron take thee
To thy master—
Felt of warnings,
Come of war-wings—

To thy parting:
God-like, hasty.

7. Sunset Song

Twa legs pivot,
Sugar bread,
Aye, we hae
A planet map
O' twa horse e'es
In darklin' skies
Where grey is gull
An' peewits[2] die
Can pick this land
Can comb thy hand
Can ride thee out
Th' earth-tilled bout
Wa' wet wa' warm
Wa' done nae harm
Wa' breath wa' bulls__t
Wa' withered full
Wa' scripted, sure,
I' th' gloamin' sky

---

[2] field birds

How to Train Your Palate to Taste French Oak as Tumbleweed Rolls By

You're so far up into the jettisoned
fractures of birch I know

the glacier doesn't give up her living.

In the paralysis of a prism you see your heart
flagless and desperately communal:
your town
is whoever withholds the most
without immolating.

It is uniquely human
to build a mining town in your lungs
just so you can name the glorious end
& pretend it wasn't imperceptible.

How to Be the Unabomber

Are you confused about pleasure too?
We've been bending like pipe-cleaner art
& hoping for a prize.

Fashions
come back every twenty years
but precedent is the enemy of revelation
so we all walk around in bad outfits.
This poem is exactly the right length.

There is the occasional accuracy of language
while you adjust your fascinator.

The bitter cleansing herbs can't get to us
through their own smoke. It's too heavy,
like the sleet that fell on the cat
that disappeared in January.

How to Become Pregnant

Just under the soloist's gaze
is a lens-shaped cloud.
It is the arc in the sky

where mountain turbulence
can kill you. Pilots patrol
the outer reaches.

Part of the arrangement is
they know little of what
they protect & maintain.

I heard Maria Callas sing
twice, once

over the noise
of a car whose driver
was trying to shake
me from his heart.

The driver's ed instructor
would have explained
that my choice
to listen at that time
threatened our well-being.

How to Disappear

If we do this anymore
It might buy the farm

And us skinny
Owls in a shed

But love, labor's only labor which
Is lost and lost only lost

Which is watched

How to Nail the D.E.C.

All the rescued yard-life
got away. I paged you

& lied when you didn't get there in time.
Where would I have started?

They called it a mountain lion and went home.

Is he moving towards the truth here?
Yeah but he's dragging his bags, said Geraldine.

We are full of unchecked deftness.

Motion sensor systems send us
mid-stride shots of fawns, the empty dark, and then

at last: seven panthers in Horseheads.

How to Regret Beauty

People missed the movement of blood,
even if it was imagined.

Predators from all walks
shed their teeth in a gesture of grief.

Everyone went home
to nurse a new reality,
except those who stayed
& walked over
& over the teeth
like spilled
grains.

Charged wi' th' Care of a Ghostflower,
One May Nae In nor Out, Speak nor Hush,
Drop nor Hold

Claret, ruby, sickle, pardon
There air nae rags a' hand.

A thicky jest, it grew itself
As resin i' th' branch-grip land.

An' turn to amber will we?
An' gem our way down down?

An' gae get dug an' dally
I' some gay chap's museum?

Nae, Duck-downy, nae, Bird-fluff
Nae, Skin-silky-hisses-bluff,

Nae, Me-armor's-rustin-through,
Nae, Sick-sorry-sudden,

Nae, Wee-shudder-cock-n-eye,
Nae, Lang-shoulder-spannin',

Nae, I shan't let aught gae down
Nae, shan't ony wine flow

Round the sickle lip o' glass
Out o' my white hand grows.

An' ho! Ye've made a bottle o' me,
Ho! I've been a flask or twa,

Ho! Who gaes tae make the pardon?—
Canna he take my Sadlove, too?

Take it tae a king, if be one,
Take it tae a queen, if dare

Take to any song that answers
I'th' briars that make all

But ne'er cry out its slight in towne
Ne'er grasp it i' th' scissoring sun

For dear thing there its stalk be split
An' a whole flow'r left for no'ne.

How to Be an Addict

I have always been
ahead of myself.

The nut-white
pill, the wild pony,

I even gave me a harp.

I've located the place
where one need not

locate anything.

In the idea you are an experience.

One sleeps
when all else

is a fisted dozen.

Why would I stay

when whole houses
can be dragged

across the ice on sledges
& reassembled?

I sleep where we know

what the land tells me

I began as.

Hop Hop Ginger

A nursery rhyme

You are a tiny ocean frog
Little shining muscle frog
Circle round and round me bouncing
Bite your tasty calf my frog!

Became a bigger beggar frog
Needer of my water frog
Hid your growing toes my frog
Now in me they're jouncing!

Free then in my pocket frog
My threadlines were your zipline frog
And thought-frog bounced away on fringe
And then frog how I back-cried-cringe!

I put you in the snow, poor frog
Sorry as a doe, face long
Big and brown of eye I sighed
But you just did a right cold-frog!

It seems I will be killing you
The honor to none other frog
My sorrow-clot is yours, sweet frog
Hop hop ginger in my sob!

How to Bomb Bridges

Remains of a bridge alarm you,
the places where people

keep coming, one mother after another
balancing across rusted beams. Someone with MS,
A drummer boy killed on Little Round Top.

They come like Darwin's pigeons rising
to a hole in the tower of the dove-cote
toward something one should never have to ask for.

How to Be Alone

Hot wind moves through
Fall's bleached palette

lying lightly over
Spring in Paso Robles.

A total of seven vines
saw their second summer. Of those,

one was lost to birds—
happy ingenuous orioles
who knew the net

was poorly draped. Their family shook
the flowering tree.

Ptarmigan

It's potent stuff, waiting. Pebbled white,
surviving by the luck of colors
your body sends out.

Language would love to truss you,
cheesecloth aping a shroud.
It's only gauze.

Let's be ready.
A falling away: Unpeopled
such that persons are possible.

It makes this specimen,
among others:
a girl wearing a muff.

I wish the molt would come
faster: the snow, the heart,
comes like disaster.

Sunsick

Hair falls
harp notes

Cut
above a
slow drain

Does not
land

Down and down a
downy, O, sigh for
a shroud

I can make
no wool

Can I have your
hairs to keep

Can I hold your
middle

Can I tell you
I'm a sheep

No then try
a fiddle

I'm quaking by
the bedrock

I'm baaing
by stacked stones

I'd gone acres, quarts
before I knew

There was no shade
in the satchel and

No shade for
the bone

How to Work in the Canyon

Carved pernambuco   placed
in careful
slots
ready for horse-hair
and violas.
    Run a finger
        over the wood
            & blooded amber flushes
        like pelicans, purposive
& endangered.

            You can make
            an instrument,
        even a tool with which to love it
        beyond reason, clear on into
frightful skill. Still
        it's at least
half   factual.

            It was a mule
        that carried them into
        the canyon
        on a trail too narrow
for its neck
to the floor

        a thousand feet
        down.

He was
a homely artless
animal cutting crystal
where there was
no room.

How to Shop from Home

Misunderstood & gorgeous,
one must rely on antiques,

subscribe to history itself as
a stunning pair of buffleheads,
which are ducks, but this time they are
doorstops.

To come to us in the winter
is as good as offering yourself smoked & dried.
Everything bleak is perfect.

Bounty begets distemper,
fooling around, & heartful bores. Stuff must be

unstuffed. Any mortician will get into his dream of Memphis
without doubting what his mind has built;

he has practiced in the hallway, the black invitation plain.
But for Wilma, there will be a coral—she loves Arizona,
the bright dust.

How to Add & Subtract

A telegram arrived
to the wrong widow
a non-widow

& then the correction note
entrapped her
with terrible fulfillments

or, the end of desire.

Back when men were men
and women were too
alive was as good as dead.

Wall

Her gesture is to trace
The wet gaps

Or to encounter the rock
Wall's rained-upon

Larvae, recoil so that

Her meander and
Her startle become

A chord.

A white pony
Munches.

Inside a stone
House a toweled hand

Pulls a tray of fish
From an oven,

Drops it.
Hot flakes rush

To the ground & spread,
Still wet.

She will never love a soldier.

Tumbling wall, posture
On which rain breaks,

In which beetles hum.

Reef

If you hate gulls they will be
Your way out
To a cold air-tank of sky. If you hate
Their gray it will bite to blue, a particular
Oblivion. If their shit gets you,
It becomes the salve
For an undying itch, or the unformed sob.
Their shape will make you leap to see
The falcon they are not,
And you'll settle back
To your boat's seat, knowing at least
(At *least* the fine spray off the bow
from no direction, from all directions)
The template was in you, like a new-hatched chick shown
The silhouette of the fiercest thing that can befall it,
Having been alive for only
Minutes, hitting the deck, still as a ruby.

How to Lay the Tracks behind the Train

Around the time you gave up ancient monoliths
I became ancient & monolithic.

I want to filter
into your crowd
of regular sunlight

like regular sunlight. In the war

you would have
made it home. I think
you would have seen ghosts.

Let me see them.

How to Get Over the Gulf

An assembly of ruby-throated hummingbirds departs
out over the Gulf   stumbles upon a headwind
& just over eight hours in
drops into the waves

almost without sound. One bird catches
an improbable eddy of wind
and, finished with its fat reserves
consumes its own muscle
to get to the bayou

drinks a thousand flowers
and lives to be   if not tell
the tale.

Someone's carelessness;
that's where the hummingbird lives.

Proxima

Whatever comes in that chariot
we must work to slow its progress, deconstruct
what's smuggled in its billow.
The parts are the sin of the whole.

Once the queen is fractal you may gather
her intonations—go ahead,
count the ways they could enter a black hole
on your one good finger.

We speak to survive, recite handwork
until sound calcifies,
the collarbone's final instrument.
Language will always prove fatal to captors.

Do you remember the violent indignity
when we tried to enter the ocean?
Shame entered our ears in the foam.
We annulled our knee-gashes
and never talked again.

How to Avoid Incineration upon Re-entry

Permit me a period of adjustment,
a time to cease asking questions
of grieving people.

Part of respecting wildlife is letting it die.
Pine pitch comes pouring out
in waves.

Someone with one foot
in the other world had the foresight
to disenchant the season

by translating it
into bad English in tiny print.
Not that you've read it.

You'll never remember
how your fingers get clean.

How to Go to Bed

A ladder of water runs downward at bedtime.
She holds the disappearances like rungs,
head at a broken angle
after the shock of each lack.

A two-tone vocalise
runs out.

The quietest time
is after the holiday, when you're sated
& not yet ready to regret.
For that you'd need your boots on.

How to Resurrect a Mammoth

Deserts have
an art of withholding.
Sort your own socks.

In the archaeologist's dream
she shakes at the return of
conviction & restraint.

Outside her tent,
the project
marches forward,

real people
its banners.

Who is keeping
the ancient

femur & pelvis
from shattering?

The team puts
down its tiny hammers

Total Agreement

1.

The Pratt & Whitney Wasp
has a human sound.

2.

Not many aphorisms survive,
& none to a tune you'd know.

3.

Atrocity stops to sing a song
in a valley full of larks.

4.

A copy of a wolf & the wolf itself
are the same if you draw them both.

How to Write a Debut Novel

You grow prolix, friend,
but never weepy. Thank you.
The great husk's imprecations
aren't enough to spit you out.
Your fibrous eyes have been
tousling the real world. There are hair-prints
in your pottery.
We omit the *u* from Mourning Doves
because the AV Club can use
their breast feathers
for a decent framing project.

That's the Way I Roll

A stream,
a lost turkey.

This isn't how you ache, it's waiting.
Assemble the great fence.
I won't turn to see who opened it

on my way to the river
where I'm supposed to drink
& continue living.

Atrocity speaks potato,
means nothing by it.
[We procreate. The End.]

I want less & less to be in present use.
Look—a hive
for pounds of winter
honey.

How to Redeploy

We saw a killing field
(a ready-to-do),

grabbed up
our handsful,

weighed rancor
& sailed out.

The demographics
of the sternum

now that they're present & sober
become a worried cross-sea,

like a race of porpoise
saving itself.

How to Abandon Prose

If you can scoop names from
your mouth like minerals
you are a quarry where one can see the earth
clear as a bedroom.

She has
an agate somewhere; there won't be an
autobiography.
She knows her collection
so well it is

no longer hers.

How to Bless the Gods

We're buying
real estate on Loi'hi,
a volcanic mound

that won't break
the surface of the Pacific
for ten thousand years.

Backstage at *Madama Butterfly*
an understudy bets that he can vanish
the most important prop

He swipes three cups in circles
& the riggers watch it happen,
that which can't be true.

How to Drown in Four Inches of Water

They lowered the lake level
before we could trailer her out off her keel
& a thousand said & unsaid things.

Where's the submersion
that would seal the summer
in a hissing lunge, like hot iron into water
leaving its color behind?

The sailboarders stay into November
with only each other's pennants
& the shallow water to criss-cross

That's how big the whole world is
punctuated by waterfowl tough as Jack Dempsey.

It turns out Mohammed Ali was really funny;
maybe we can watch that documentary.
I never wanted to love anything
more than your swanky frame.

How to Take the Easy Way Out

The truck & the building
join

at the divided by line.

They remain hulking, stone enough
to look Rome in the eye & spit.

This is the way
of the mountain. It slips into town

on a bad afternoon.
Routine is impossible.
We can see the crashing in,

the bricks' emphasis
on death and dust,

we understand the stunned
articulation of a bare spine.

How to Go Extinct

for the Ivory-billed Woodpecker

Cecil's kints took up a lot of time. Why couldn't
a grown man pack it in? People sat on his porch
trying to find out and left with a story about a mule.
He had every drawing of the peckerwood anyone
could have. Cecil knew Rod Billings shot some in
the twenties, a mated pair, & never found the tree
again to see if there was a nest. The skins got him
cash from a collector & a piece in the paper. Cecil
heard the truck gutter out & his head filled with
static. Up to his neck in swamp he sometimes saw
incisions in the sky faster than a wood duck & felt
the back of his eyeballs go cold with the effort &
desire.

How to Find the Labor Day Fair

I am at the Labor Day fair
three boys tracking me
I'm pretty sure.

I only barely know
I'm in the swamp
where

a long time from now
the extinct
will rise
easy as martins
into the world

How to Dissect a Bird

for Jim Galvin

Red-winged blackbirds slit their wrists
in February
so we don't have to.

No wonder they sound
like rust. One time
someone dared me to stop every line at its end.

People resist like it's
the fright of color
in a ditch.

No one talks about
how to spell, how our hands
are in charge of our hearts.

I couldn't find
the many organs,
even taken out of the hawk—

they were all
one thing, far
as I could tell.

However Full We May Seem

---

knowledge dolphins through us
like shrapnel
through   deer.

In the A-frame, a projector
flickers. All is not   gathered.

I jury-rig the truck.

We are capable of
                    waiting.

If you must

be a planet, O,
                    stand

near
        the house

Ithaka

for Martha, the last known Passenger Pigeon, d. Sept. 1st, 1914

I'm rolling in the truck bed
wound in wire.
I can't recall any jokes

so it seems I shouldn't be
naked. Across the trestle, low as a grouse,
one hears rumors of freight.

The spring crow grows strong;
the hoarders' hands
flutter & chime with coin.

"I want more,"
said the great Odysseus.
The singer has forgotten that,

& many other parts
of this song.

Acknowledgments

Thank you to the following publications, where poems from this manuscript originally appeared:

Colorado Review
Conduit
Devil's Lake
H_NGM_N
Seneca Review
Sixth Finch

Thank you also especially to Sam Dean, Margaret Manring, Jim Galvin, Dean Young, Deborah Tall, David Weiss, Cole Swensen, Seth Abramson, Julia Green, Katherine Klein, Emily Dean, and Dwight Swift for your help and encouragement

Also from The National Poetry Review Press

Lucktown by Bryan Penberthy

Bill's Formal Complaint by Dan Kaplan

Gilgamesh at the Bellagio by Karl Elder

Legend of the Recent Past by James Haug

Urchin to Follow by Dorine Jennette

The Kissing Party by Sarah E. Barber

Deepening Groove by Ravi Shankar

The City from Nome by James Grinwis

Fort Gorgeous by Angela Vogel

Able, Baker, Charlie by John Mann

The Wanted by Michael Tyrell

Loud Dreaming in a Quiet Room by Betsy Wheeler

Guest Host by Elizabeth Hughey

Inside the Color of Water by Lynne Potts

Please visit our website for more information:

www.nationalpoetryreview.com

CPSIA information can be obtained at www.ICGtesting.com
Printed in the USA
BVOW08s1251110214

344589BV00001B/8/P